FOOD
Diary

Daily Diary To Track Diet And Symptoms To Beat
Food Intolerances And Digestive Disorders

First published in 2018 by Erin Rose Publishing

Text and illustration copyright © 2018 Erin Rose Publishing

Design: Julie Anson

ISBN: 978-1-911492-20-7

A CIP record for this book is available from the British Library.

DISCLAIMER: This book is not intended as a substitute for the medical advice, diagnosis or treatment by a physician or qualified healthcare provider.

Introduction

Welcome to your food diary!

Working out what foods may be causing health issues, such as digestive symptoms can be confusing. To help you find out which foods are causing you problems we have created this specially designed food diary. By using this book daily, you can log all the essential information, including what you eat and what symptoms you experience, to identify food intolerances and allergies which can cause bloating, indigestion, weight gain, skin complaints and IBS.

It's really simple to use. You can get started straight away by completing the relevant sections for all important information, so you can quickly and easily start building up a clear picture of your diet, health and well-being. Use this diary to record exactly what you eat and how you feel and you will very quickly identify patterns.

You will able to avoid foods which trigger symptoms and take positive steps towards improving your health and well-being. This food diary helps you work towards discovering and completing the section 'Your Go-Ahead List'.

This food diary contains 3 months of journal pages for you to fill out and record information like, diet, calorie intake, medication, supplements, fluid intake, calories, stress levels and bowel action, helping you understand how your diet is affecting you.

How To Use Your Food Diary

To enable you to record accurately, make an entry in your food diary every time you eat, so keep it with you if you are on-the-go. It is much easier than reflecting back on the day.

Simply fill out all the sections and write down your food intake - even the little snacks. Complete all the comprehensive sections and remember to write down how you feel, paying particular attention to digestive reactions such as bloating and indigestion. Based on whether a food has triggered a reaction, you can tick the relevant box and go on to complete the section at the rear of this book to compile your own personal 'avoid' and 'go-ahead' list providing you with a valuable record of your unique dietary requirements.

Sometimes after avoiding a foodstuff for a period of time you will be able to re-introduce it at a later date and not suffer any reaction. This is only the case in food intolerances and not allergies. If you have known allergies it is important to continue avoiding these. If you suffer symptoms such as shortness of breath, vomiting, throat and/or tongue swelling, dizziness or an itchy rash, seek medical attention straight away. Likewise with any persistent or recurring health issues, you should seek your doctor's advice.

Wishing you great health!

Daily Food Diary

Date: . . . .

Time	🍲 Food & Quantity Consumed	Calories	Symptoms: No ✗/Yes ✓

	Supplements	Medication	Dosage

Symptoms Description	Scale 1-10

Stress Level (Tick one)		Fluid Intake	Caffeine Intake	Bowel Action
☺				
😐				
☹				

Daily Food Diary

Date: . . . .

Time	🍲 Food & Quantity Consumed	Calories	Symptoms: No ⊗ /Yes ✓

	Supplements	Medication	Dosage

Symptoms Description	Scale 1-10

Stress Level (Tick one)		Fluid Intake	Caffeine Intake	Bowel Action
☺				
😐				
☹				

Daily Food Diary

Date: . . . .

Time	🍲 Food & Quantity Consumed	Calories	Symptoms: No ✗ / Yes ✓

Supplements	Medication	Dosage

Symptoms Description	Scale 1-10

Stress Level (Tick one)	Fluid Intake	Caffeine Intake	Bowel Action
☺			
☹			
☹			

Daily Food Diary

Date: . . . .

Time	🍲 Food & Quantity Consumed	Calories	Symptoms: No ✗/Yes ✓

	Supplements	Medication	Dosage

Symptoms Description	Scale 1-10

Stress Level (Tick one)		Fluid Intake	Caffeine Intake	Bowel Action
☺				
😐				
☹				

Daily Food Diary

Date: . . . .

Time	🍲 Food & Quantity Consumed	Calories	Symptoms: No ⊗/Yes ✓

	Supplements	Medication	Dosage

Symptoms Description	Scale 1-10

Stress Level (Tick one)		Fluid Intake	Caffeine Intake	Bowel Action
☺				
😐				
☹				

Daily Food Diary

Date: . . . .

Time	🍲 Food & Quantity Consumed	Calories	Symptoms: No ✗/Yes ✓

	Supplements	Medication	Dosage

Symptoms Description	Scale 1-10

Stress Level (Tick one)		Fluid Intake	Caffeine Intake	Bowel Action
☺				
😐				
☹				

Daily Food Diary

Date: . . . .

Time	🍲 Food & Quantity Consumed	Calories	Symptoms: No ✖/Yes ✔

	Supplements	Medication	Dosage

Symptoms Description	Scale 1-10

Stress Level (Tick one)	Fluid Intake	Caffeine Intake	Bowel Action
☺			
😐			
☹			

Daily Food Diary

Date: ....

Time	🍲 Food & Quantity Consumed	Calories	Symptoms: No ⊗/Yes ✓

	Supplements	Medication	Dosage

Symptoms Description	Scale 1-10

Stress Level (Tick one)		Fluid Intake	Caffeine Intake	Bowel Action
☺				
😐				
☹				

Daily Food Diary

Date: . . . .

Time	🥣 Food & Quantity Consumed	Calories	Symptoms: No ✖/Yes ✔

	Supplements	Medication	Dosage

Symptoms Description	Scale 1-10

Stress Level (Tick one)		Fluid Intake	Caffeine Intake	Bowel Action
☺				
😐				
☹				

Daily Food Diary

Date: . . . .

Time	🍲 Food & Quantity Consumed	Calories	Symptoms: No ⊗ / Yes ✓

	Supplements	Medication	Dosage

Symptoms Description	Scale 1-10

Stress Level (Tick one)		Fluid Intake	Caffeine Intake	Bowel Action
☺				
😐				
☹				

Daily Food Diary

Date: . . . .

Time	🍲 Food & Quantity Consumed	Calories	Symptoms: No ✖/Yes ✔

	Supplements	Medication	Dosage

Symptoms Description	Scale 1-10

Stress Level (Tick one)	Fluid Intake	Caffeine Intake	Bowel Action
🙂			
😐			
🙁			

Daily Food Diary

Date: . . . .

Time	🍲 Food & Quantity Consumed	Calories	Symptoms: No ⊗/Yes ✓

	Supplements	Medication	Dosage

Symptoms Description	Scale 1-10

Stress Level (Tick one)		Fluid Intake	Caffeine Intake	Bowel Action
☺				
😐				
☹				

Daily Food Diary

Date: . . . .

Time	🍲 Food & Quantity Consumed	Calories	Symptoms: No ✗/Yes ✓

Supplements	Medication	Dosage

Symptoms Description	Scale 1-10

Stress Level (Tick one)		Fluid Intake	Caffeine Intake	Bowel Action
☺				
😐				
☹				

Daily Food Diary

Date: ....

Time	🍲 Food & Quantity Consumed	Calories	Symptoms: No ⊗/Yes ✓

	Supplements	Medication	Dosage

Symptoms Description	Scale 1-10

Stress Level (Tick one)		Fluid Intake	Caffeine Intake	Bowel Action
☺				
😐				
☹				

Daily Food Diary

Date: . . . .

Time	🍲 Food & Quantity Consumed	Calories	Symptoms: No ✗ /Yes ✓

Supplements	Medication	Dosage

Symptoms Description	Scale 1-10

Stress Level (Tick one)		Fluid Intake	Caffeine Intake	Bowel Action
☺				
☹				
☹				

Daily Food Diary

Date: ....

Time	🍲 Food & Quantity Consumed	Calories	Symptoms: No ⊗/Yes ✓

	Supplements	Medication	Dosage

Symptoms Description	Scale 1-10

Stress Level (Tick one)		Fluid Intake	Caffeine Intake	Bowel Action
☺				
😐				
☹				

Daily Food Diary

Date: . . . .

Time	🍲 Food & Quantity Consumed	Calories	Symptoms: No ✗/Yes ✓

	Supplements	Medication	Dosage

Symptoms Description	Scale 1-10

Stress Level (Tick one)	Fluid Intake	Caffeine Intake	Bowel Action
☺			
😐			
☹			

Daily Food Diary

Date: . . . .

Time	🍲 Food & Quantity Consumed	Calories	Symptoms: No ✖/Yes ✓

	Supplements	Medication	Dosage

Symptoms Description	Scale 1-10

Stress Level (Tick one)		Fluid Intake	Caffeine Intake	Bowel Action
☺				
😐				
☹				

Daily Food Diary

Date: . . . .

Time	🍲 Food & Quantity Consumed	Calories	Symptoms: No ✗ /Yes ✓

	Supplements	Medication	Dosage

Symptoms Description	Scale 1-10

Stress Level (Tick one)		Fluid Intake	Caffeine Intake	Bowel Action
☺				
😐				
☹				

Daily Food Diary

Date: ....

Time	🍲 Food & Quantity Consumed	Calories	Symptoms: No ✗/Yes ✓

	Supplements	Medication	Dosage

Symptoms Description	Scale 1-10

Stress Level (Tick one)		Fluid Intake	Caffeine Intake	Bowel Action
☺				
😐				
☹				

Daily Food Diary

Date: . . . .

Time	🍲 Food & Quantity Consumed	Calories	Symptoms: No ⊗/Yes ✓

	Supplements	Medication	Dosage

Symptoms Description	Scale 1-10

Stress Level (Tick one)	Fluid Intake	Caffeine Intake	Bowel Action
🙂			
😐			
☹️			

Daily Food Diary

Date: . . . .

Time	🍲 Food & Quantity Consumed	Calories	Symptoms: No ✗ /Yes ✓

	Supplements	Medication	Dosage

Symptoms Description	Scale 1-10

Stress Level (Tick one)		Fluid Intake	Caffeine Intake	Bowel Action
🙂				
😐				
☹️				

Daily Food Diary

Date: . . . .

Time	Food & Quantity Consumed	Calories	Symptoms: No ✗/Yes ✓
	Supplements	Medication	Dosage

Symptoms Description	Scale 1-10

Stress Level (Tick one)	Fluid Intake	Caffeine Intake	Bowel Action
☺			
☹			
☹			

Daily Food Diary

Date: . . . .

Time	🍜 Food & Quantity Consumed	Calories	Symptoms: No ⊗/Yes ✓

	Supplements	Medication	Dosage

Symptoms Description	Scale 1-10

Stress Level (Tick one)		Fluid Intake	Caffeine Intake	Bowel Action
☺				
😐				
☹				

Daily Food Diary

Date: . . . .

Time	🥣 Food & Quantity Consumed	Calories	Symptoms: No ⊗/Yes ✓

	Supplements	Medication	Dosage

Symptoms Description	Scale 1-10

Stress Level (Tick one)		Fluid Intake	Caffeine Intake	Bowel Action
☺				
😐				
☹				

Daily Food Diary

Date: ....

Time	🥣 Food & Quantity Consumed	Calories	Symptoms: No ⊗/Yes ✓

	Supplements	Medication	Dosage

Symptoms Description	Scale 1-10

Stress Level (Tick one)		Fluid Intake	Caffeine Intake	Bowel Action
☺				
😐				
☹				

Daily Food Diary

Date: . . . .

Time	🍲 Food & Quantity Consumed	Calories	Symptoms: No ✖/Yes ✓

	Supplements	Medication	Dosage

Symptoms Description	Scale 1-10

Stress Level (Tick one)	Fluid Intake	Caffeine Intake	Bowel Action
☺			
😐			
☹			

Daily Food Diary

Date: ....

Time	🍲 Food & Quantity Consumed	Calories	Symptoms: No ✖/Yes ✔

	Supplements	Medication	Dosage

Symptoms Description	Scale 1-10

Stress Level (Tick one)		Fluid Intake	Caffeine Intake	Bowel Action
😊				
😐				
☹				

Daily Food Diary

Date: . . . .

Time	🍲 Food & Quantity Consumed	Calories	Symptoms: No ✖/Yes ✔

	Supplements	Medication	Dosage

Symptoms Description	Scale 1-10

Stress Level (Tick one)		Fluid Intake	Caffeine Intake	Bowel Action
☺				
😐				
☹				

Daily Food Diary

Date: . . . .

Time	🍜 Food & Quantity Consumed	Calories	Symptoms: No ⊗ /Yes ✓

	Supplements	Medication	Dosage

Symptoms Description	Scale 1-10

Stress Level (Tick one)		Fluid Intake	Caffeine Intake	Bowel Action
☺				
😐				
☹				

Daily Food Diary

Date: . . . .

Time	Food & Quantity Consumed	Calories	Symptoms: No ✗/Yes ✓

	Supplements	Medication	Dosage

Symptoms Description	Scale 1-10

Stress Level (Tick one)		Fluid Intake	Caffeine Intake	Bowel Action
☺				
☹				
☹				

Daily Food Diary

Date: . . . .

Time	🍲 Food & Quantity Consumed	Calories	Symptoms: No ✖/Yes ✓

	Supplements	Medication	Dosage

Symptoms Description	Scale 1-10

Stress Level (Tick one)		Fluid Intake	Caffeine Intake	Bowel Action
🙂				
😐				
🙁				

Daily Food Diary

Date: . . . .

Time	🍲 Food & Quantity Consumed	Calories	Symptoms: No ✗/Yes ✓

	Supplements	Medication	Dosage

Symptoms Description	Scale 1-10

Stress Level (Tick one)		Fluid Intake	Caffeine Intake	Bowel Action
☺				
😐				
☹				

Daily Food Diary

Date: . . . .

Time	🍜 Food & Quantity Consumed	Calories	Symptoms: No ✖ /Yes ✔

	Supplements	Medication	Dosage

Symptoms Description	Scale 1-10

Stress Level (Tick one)		Fluid Intake	Caffeine Intake	Bowel Action
🙂				
😐				
☹️				

Daily Food Diary

Date: . . . .

Time	🍲 Food & Quantity Consumed	Calories	Symptoms: No ⊗/Yes ✓

Supplements	Medication	Dosage

Symptoms Description	Scale 1-10

Stress Level (Tick one)	Fluid Intake	Caffeine Intake	Bowel Action
☺			
😐			
☹			

Daily Food Diary

Date: . . . .

Time	☕ Food & Quantity Consumed	Calories	Symptoms: No ✗/Yes ✓

	Supplements	Medication	Dosage

Symptoms Description	Scale 1-10

Stress Level (Tick one)		Fluid Intake	Caffeine Intake	Bowel Action
☺				
😐				
☹				

Daily Food Diary

Date: . . . .

Time	🥣 Food & Quantity Consumed	Calories	Symptoms: No ✖/Yes ✔

	Supplements	Medication	Dosage

Symptoms Description	Scale 1-10

Stress Level (Tick one)		Fluid Intake	Caffeine Intake	Bowel Action
☺				
😐				
☹				

Daily Food Diary

Date: . . . .

Time	🥣 Food & Quantity Consumed	Calories	Symptoms: No ⊗/Yes ✓

	Supplements	Medication	Dosage

Symptoms Description	Scale 1-10

Stress Level (Tick one)		Fluid Intake	Caffeine Intake	Bowel Action
☺				
😐				
☹				

Daily Food Diary

Date: . . . .

Time	🍲 Food & Quantity Consumed	Calories	Symptoms: No ✗/Yes ✓

	Supplements	Medication	Dosage

Symptoms Description	Scale 1-10

Stress Level (Tick one)	Fluid Intake	Caffeine Intake	Bowel Action
☺			
😐			
☹			

Daily Food Diary

Date: . . . .

Time	🍲 Food & Quantity Consumed	Calories	Symptoms: No ⊗/Yes ✓

	Supplements	Medication	Dosage

Symptoms Description	Scale 1-10

Stress Level (Tick one)		Fluid Intake	Caffeine Intake	Bowel Action
☺				
😐				
☹				

Daily Food Diary

Date: . . . .

Time	🥣 Food & Quantity Consumed	Calories	Symptoms: No ⊗/Yes ✓

	Supplements	Medication	Dosage

Symptoms Description	Scale 1-10

Stress Level (Tick one)		Fluid Intake	Caffeine Intake	Bowel Action
☺				
😐				
☹				

Daily Food Diary

Date: ....

Time	🍲 Food & Quantity Consumed	Calories	Symptoms: No ✖/Yes ✔

	Supplements	Medication	Dosage

Symptoms Description	Scale 1-10

Stress Level (Tick one)		Fluid Intake	Caffeine Intake	Bowel Action
☺				
😐				
☹				

Daily Food Diary

Date: . . . .

Time	🍲 Food & Quantity Consumed	Calories	Symptoms: No ⊗/Yes ✓
	Supplements	Medication	Dosage

Symptoms Description	Scale 1-10

Stress Level (Tick one)	Fluid Intake	Caffeine Intake	Bowel Action
☺			
😐			
☹			

Daily Food Diary

Date: . . . .

Time	🍲 Food & Quantity Consumed	Calories	Symptoms: No ✗/Yes ✓

	Supplements	Medication	Dosage

Symptoms Description	Scale 1-10

Stress Level (Tick one)		Fluid Intake	Caffeine Intake	Bowel Action
☺				
😐				
☹				

Daily Food Diary

Date: . . . .

Time	🥣 Food & Quantity Consumed	Calories	Symptoms: No ✖/Yes ✔

	Supplements	Medication	Dosage

Symptoms Description	Scale 1-10

Stress Level (Tick one)	Fluid Intake	Caffeine Intake	Bowel Action
☺			
😐			
☹			

Daily Food Diary

Date: . . . .

Time	🍲 Food & Quantity Consumed	Calories	Symptoms: No ⊗/Yes ✓

	Supplements	Medication	Dosage

Symptoms Description	Scale 1-10

Stress Level (Tick one)		Fluid Intake	Caffeine Intake	Bowel Action
☺				
☺				
☹				

Daily Food Diary

Date: . . . .

Time	🍲 Food & Quantity Consumed	Calories	Symptoms: No ⊗/Yes ✓

	Supplements	Medication	Dosage

Symptoms Description	Scale 1-10

Stress Level (Tick one)		Fluid Intake	Caffeine Intake	Bowel Action
☺				
😐				
☹				

Daily Food Diary

Date: . . . .

Time	🍲 Food & Quantity Consumed	Calories	Symptoms: No ⊗/Yes ✓

	Supplements	Medication	Dosage

Symptoms Description	Scale 1-10

Stress Level (Tick one)		Fluid Intake	Caffeine Intake	Bowel Action
☺				
😐				
☹				

Daily Food Diary

Date: . . . .

Time	🍲 Food & Quantity Consumed	Calories	Symptoms: No ⊗/Yes ✓

	Supplements	Medication	Dosage

Symptoms Description	Scale 1-10

Stress Level (Tick one)		Fluid Intake	Caffeine Intake	Bowel Action
☺				
😐				
☹				

Daily Food Diary

Date: . . . .

Time	🍲 Food & Quantity Consumed	Calories	Symptoms: No ✗/Yes ✓

	Supplements	Medication	Dosage

Symptoms Description	Scale 1-10

Stress Level (Tick one)		Fluid Intake	Caffeine Intake	Bowel Action
☺				
😐				
☹				

Daily Food Diary

Date: . . . .

Time	🍲 Food & Quantity Consumed	Calories	Symptoms: No ✗/Yes ✓

	Supplements	Medication	Dosage

Symptoms Description	Scale 1-10

Stress Level (Tick one)		Fluid Intake	Caffeine Intake	Bowel Action
🙂				
😐				
☹️				

Daily Food Diary

Date: . . . .

Time	🍲 Food & Quantity Consumed	Calories	Symptoms: No ⊗/Yes ✓

	Supplements	Medication	Dosage

Symptoms Description	Scale 1-10

Stress Level (Tick one)		Fluid Intake	Caffeine Intake	Bowel Action
☺				
😐				
☹				

Daily Food Diary

Date: . . . .

Time	🍲 Food & Quantity Consumed	Calories	Symptoms: No ✗/Yes ✓

	Supplements	Medication	Dosage

Symptoms Description	Scale 1-10

Stress Level (Tick one)		Fluid Intake	Caffeine Intake	Bowel Action
☺				
😐				
☹				

Daily Food Diary

Date: . . . .

Time	🥣 Food & Quantity Consumed	Calories	Symptoms: No ✗/Yes ✓

	Supplements	Medication	Dosage

Symptoms Description	Scale 1-10

Stress Level (Tick one)		Fluid Intake	Caffeine Intake	Bowel Action
☺				
😐				
☹				

Daily Food Diary

Date: . . . .

Time	🍲 Food & Quantity Consumed	Calories	Symptoms: No ⊗ /Yes ✓

Supplements	Medication	Dosage

Symptoms Description	Scale 1-10

Stress Level (Tick one)	Fluid Intake	Caffeine Intake	Bowel Action
☺			
😐			
☹			

Daily Food Diary

Date: . . . .

Time	🍜 Food & Quantity Consumed	Calories	Symptoms: No ⊗/Yes ✓

	Supplements	Medication	Dosage

Symptoms Description	Scale 1-10

Stress Level (Tick one)		Fluid Intake	Caffeine Intake	Bowel Action
☺				
😐				
☹				

Daily Food Diary

Date: ....

Time	🍲 Food & Quantity Consumed	Calories	Symptoms: No ⊗/Yes ✓

	Supplements	Medication	Dosage

Symptoms Description	Scale 1-10

Stress Level (Tick one)	Fluid Intake	Caffeine Intake	Bowel Action
☺			
😐			
☹			

Daily Food Diary

Date: . . . .

Time	🍲 Food & Quantity Consumed	Calories	Symptoms: No ⊗/Yes ✓

	Supplements	Medication	Dosage

Symptoms Description	Scale 1-10

Stress Level (Tick one)		Fluid Intake	Caffeine Intake	Bowel Action
☺				
😐				
☹				

Daily Food Diary

Date: . . . .

Time	🍲 Food & Quantity Consumed	Calories	Symptoms: No ✗/Yes ✓

	Supplements	Medication	Dosage

Symptoms Description	Scale 1-10

Stress Level (Tick one)	Fluid Intake	Caffeine Intake	Bowel Action
☺			
😐			
☹			

Daily Food Diary

Date: . . . .

Time	🍲 Food & Quantity Consumed	Calories	Symptoms: No ⊗/Yes ✓

	Supplements	Medication	Dosage

Symptoms Description	Scale 1-10

Stress Level (Tick one)		Fluid Intake	Caffeine Intake	Bowel Action
☺				
😐				
☹				

Daily Food Diary

Date: . . . .

Time	🍲 Food & Quantity Consumed	Calories	Symptoms: No ✗/Yes ✓

Supplements	Medication	Dosage

Symptoms Description	Scale 1-10

Stress Level (Tick one)		Fluid Intake	Caffeine Intake	Bowel Action
😊				
😐				
☹️				

Daily Food Diary

Date: . . . .

Time	🍲 Food & Quantity Consumed	Calories	Symptoms: No ⊗/Yes ✓

	Supplements	Medication	Dosage

Symptoms Description	Scale 1-10

Stress Level (Tick one)		Fluid Intake	Caffeine Intake	Bowel Action
☺				
😐				
☹				

Daily Food Diary

Date: . . . .

Time	🥣 Food & Quantity Consumed	Calories	Symptoms: No ✗ /Yes ✓

	Supplements	Medication	Dosage

Symptoms Description	Scale 1-10

Stress Level (Tick one)		Fluid Intake	Caffeine Intake	Bowel Action
☺				
😐				
☹				

Daily Food Diary

Date: . . . .

Time	🍲 Food & Quantity Consumed	Calories	Symptoms: No ⊗/Yes ☑

	Supplements	Medication	Dosage

Symptoms Description	Scale 1-10

Stress Level (Tick one)		Fluid Intake	Caffeine Intake	Bowel Action
☺				
😐				
☹				

Daily Food Diary

Date: . . . .

Time	🍲 Food & Quantity Consumed	Calories	Symptoms: No ✗/Yes ✓

	Supplements	Medication	Dosage

Symptoms Description	Scale 1-10

Stress Level (Tick one)		Fluid Intake	Caffeine Intake	Bowel Action
☺				
😐				
☹				

Daily Food Diary

Date: . . . .

Time	🍲 Food & Quantity Consumed	Calories	Symptoms: No ✖/Yes ✓

	Supplements	Medication	Dosage

Symptoms Description	Scale 1-10

Stress Level (Tick one)	Fluid Intake	Caffeine Intake	Bowel Action
☺			
😐			
☹			

Daily Food Diary

Date: . . . .

Time	🍲 Food & Quantity Consumed	Calories	Symptoms: No ✗/Yes ✓

	Supplements	Medication	Dosage

Symptoms Description	Scale 1-10

Stress Level (Tick one)		Fluid Intake	Caffeine Intake	Bowel Action
☺				
😐				
☹				

Daily Food Diary

Date: . . . .

Time	🥣 Food & Quantity Consumed	Calories	Symptoms: No ⊗/Yes ✓

	Supplements	Medication	Dosage

Symptoms Description	Scale 1-10

Stress Level (Tick one)		Fluid Intake	Caffeine Intake	Bowel Action
🙂				
😐				
🙁				

Daily Food Diary

Date: . . . .

Time	🍲 Food & Quantity Consumed	Calories	Symptoms: No ✖/Yes ✔

	Supplements	Medication	Dosage

Symptoms Description	Scale 1-10

Stress Level (Tick one)		Fluid Intake	Caffeine Intake	Bowel Action
🙂				
😐				
🙁				

Daily Food Diary

Date: . . . .

Time	🍲 Food & Quantity Consumed	Calories	Symptoms: No ✖/Yes ✓

	Supplements	Medication	Dosage

Symptoms Description	Scale 1-10

Stress Level (Tick one)	Fluid Intake	Caffeine Intake	Bowel Action
☺			
😐			
☹			

Daily Food Diary

Date: . . . .

Time	🍲 Food & Quantity Consumed	Calories	Symptoms: No ⊗/Yes ✓

	Supplements	Medication	Dosage

Symptoms Description	Scale 1-10

Stress Level (Tick one)		Fluid Intake	Caffeine Intake	Bowel Action
🙂				
😐				
☹️				

Daily Food Diary

Date: . . . .

Time	🍲 Food & Quantity Consumed	Calories	Symptoms: No ✗/Yes ✓

	Supplements	Medication	Dosage

Symptoms Description	Scale 1-10

Stress Level (Tick one)		Fluid Intake	Caffeine Intake	Bowel Action
😊				
😐				
😞				

Daily Food Diary

Date: . . . .

Time	🍲 Food & Quantity Consumed	Calories	Symptoms: No ⊗/Yes ✓

Supplements	Medication	Dosage

Symptoms Description	Scale 1-10

Stress Level (Tick one)	Fluid Intake	Caffeine Intake	Bowel Action
☺			
😐			
☹			

Daily Food Diary

Date: . . . .

Time	🍲 Food & Quantity Consumed	Calories	Symptoms: No ⊗/Yes ✓

	Supplements	Medication	Dosage

Symptoms Description	Scale 1-10

Stress Level (Tick one)		Fluid Intake	Caffeine Intake	Bowel Action
☺				
😐				
☹				

Daily Food Diary

Date: . . . .

Time	🍲 Food & Quantity Consumed	Calories	Symptoms: No ⊗/Yes ✓

	Supplements	Medication	Dosage

Symptoms Description	Scale 1-10

Stress Level (Tick one)		Fluid Intake	Caffeine Intake	Bowel Action
☺				
😐				
☹				

Daily Food Diary

Date: . . . .

Time	🥣 Food & Quantity Consumed	Calories	Symptoms: No ✗/Yes ✓

	Supplements	Medication	Dosage

Symptoms Description	Scale 1-10

Stress Level (Tick one)		Fluid Intake	Caffeine Intake	Bowel Action
☺				
😐				
☹				

Daily Food Diary

Date: . . . .

Time	🍲 Food & Quantity Consumed	Calories	Symptoms: No ✗/Yes ✓

	Supplements	Medication	Dosage

Symptoms Description	Scale 1-10

Stress Level (Tick one)	Fluid Intake	Caffeine Intake	Bowel Action
☺				
😐				
☹				

Daily Food Diary

Date: . . . .

Time	🍲 Food & Quantity Consumed	Calories	Symptoms: No ⊗/Yes ✓

	Supplements	Medication	Dosage

Symptoms Description	Scale 1-10

Stress Level (Tick one)	Fluid Intake	Caffeine Intake	Bowel Action
☺			
😐			
☹			

Daily Food Diary

Date: . . . .

Time	🍲 Food & Quantity Consumed	Calories	Symptoms: No ✗/Yes ✓

	Supplements	Medication	Dosage

Symptoms Description	Scale 1-10

Stress Level (Tick one)	Fluid Intake	Caffeine Intake	Bowel Action
☺			
😐			
☹			

Daily Food Diary

Date: . . . .

Time	🍲 Food & Quantity Consumed	Calories	Symptoms: No ⊗ /Yes ✓

	Supplements	Medication	Dosage

Symptoms Description	Scale 1-10

Stress Level (Tick one)		Fluid Intake	Caffeine Intake	Bowel Action
☺				
😐				
☹				

Daily Food Diary

Date: . . . .

Time	🍲 Food & Quantity Consumed	Calories	Symptoms: No ✗/Yes ✓

	Supplements	Medication	Dosage

Symptoms Description	Scale 1-10

Stress Level (Tick one)	Fluid Intake	Caffeine Intake	Bowel Action
🙂			
😐			
☹️			

Daily Food Diary

Date: . . . .

Time	🍲 Food & Quantity Consumed	Calories	Symptoms: No ✗ /Yes ✓

	Supplements	Medication	Dosage

Symptoms Description	Scale 1-10

Stress Level (Tick one)		Fluid Intake	Caffeine Intake	Bowel Action
😊				
😐				
😞				

Daily Food Diary

Date: . . . .

Time	Food & Quantity Consumed	Calories	Symptoms: No ✗ / Yes ✓

Supplements	Medication	Dosage

Symptoms Description	Scale 1-10

Stress Level (Tick one)		Fluid Intake	Caffeine Intake	Bowel Action
☺				
😐				
☹				

Daily Food Diary

Date: . . . .

Time	🍲 Food & Quantity Consumed	Calories	Symptoms: No ⊗/Yes ✓

	Supplements	Medication	Dosage

Symptoms Description	Scale 1-10

Stress Level (Tick one)		Fluid Intake	Caffeine Intake	Bowel Action
☺				
😐				
☹				

Daily Food Diary

Date: . . . .

Time	🍲 Food & Quantity Consumed	Calories	Symptoms: No ⊗/Yes ✓

	Supplements	Medication	Dosage

Symptoms Description	Scale 1-10

Stress Level (Tick one)		Fluid Intake	Caffeine Intake	Bowel Action
☺				
😐				
☹				

Daily Food Diary

Date: . . . .

Time	🍲 Food & Quantity Consumed	Calories	Symptoms: No ⊗/Yes ✓

	Supplements	Medication	Dosage

Symptoms Description	Scale 1-10

Stress Level (Tick one)		Fluid Intake	Caffeine Intake	Bowel Action
☺				
😐				
☹				

Daily Food Diary

Date: . . . .

Time	🍲 Food & Quantity Consumed	Calories	Symptoms: No ✗/Yes ✓

Supplements	Medication	Dosage

Symptoms Description	Scale 1-10

Stress Level (Tick one)	Fluid Intake	Caffeine Intake	Bowel Action
☺			
😐			
☹			

Daily Food Diary

Date: ....

Time	🍲 Food & Quantity Consumed	Calories	Symptoms: No ⊗/Yes ✓

	Supplements	Medication	Dosage

Symptoms Description	Scale 1-10

Stress Level (Tick one)		Fluid Intake	Caffeine Intake	Bowel Action
☺				
😐				
☹				

Daily Food Diary

Date: . . . .

Time	🍲 Food & Quantity Consumed	Calories	Symptoms: No ⊗/Yes ✓

	Supplements	Medication	Dosage

Symptoms Description	Scale 1-10

Stress Level (Tick one)		Fluid Intake	Caffeine Intake	Bowel Action
☺				
😐				
☹				

Daily Food Diary

Date: . . . .

Time	⏲ Food & Quantity Consumed	Calories	Symptoms: No ⊗ /Yes ✓

	Supplements	Medication	Dosage

Symptoms Description	Scale 1-10

Stress Level (Tick one)		Fluid Intake	Caffeine Intake	Bowel Action
☺				
😐				
☹				

Your Personal AVOID list

Quantity	Food	Symptoms caused Scale 1-10	Date

⊗ Your Personal AVOID list

Quantity	Food	Symptoms caused Scale 1-10	Date

Your Personal AVOID list

Quantity	Food	Symptoms caused Scale 1-10	Date

Your Personal GO AHEAD list

Quantity	Food	Date

Your Personal GO AHEAD list

Quantity	Food	Date

Your Personal GO AHEAD list

Quantity	Food	Date

Made in the USA
San Bernardino, CA
26 July 2020